Which Family Member Would You Want to Be?

by Mrs. Clausen-Grac
and Ms. Mikkelson's clas
with Tony Stead

capstone

Introduction

by Kaytlyn

Have you ever wondered what life is like in other families? No family is the same, but they all have something in common: Everyone has jobs to do. Our classes learned about family roles throughout history, in other places, and right here in Florida and Illinois. Read on to learn about different roles in different kinds of families.

illustrated by Lauren

Families Living and Surviving in Colonial Times

by Angel

Colonial times in the United States lasted from 1492 to 1800 when people colonized, or built settlements on land they lived on. It was hard for families to live in colonial times. They had to build their own homes and plant their own food. In order to survive, every family member had a job to do.

There was usually a dad, mom, and children in the family. The father worked outdoors, crafting, hunting, and building a house to live in. He helped his family survive.

The mother of the family worked in the home. She cooked, cleaned, and made clothes. She also took care of the children. She provided for the family, too.

The son hunted and fished liked the father. Some sons were apprentices. This means that they learned how to do things like blacksmith, make wheels, bake bread, or print newspapers.

The daughter cooked, cleaned, made clothes, and picked vegetables in the garden. She also helped the mom care for other children in the family.

In colonial times, every family member had to work hard. From hunting to cooking, family members did all that they could to help each other.

Families on the Oregon Trail

by Lauren

In the late 1800s, many families risked their lives going on a dangerous journey. It was worth it. They traveled west on the Oregon Trail so they could make a new life. They learned about free land in the west from brave explorers who had been there and brought stories back about their travels. The 2,000-mile long Oregon Trail started in Independence, Missouri.

Thousands of people went on the Oregon Trail. They all came from various places. The families had babies, children, teenagers, adults, and sometimes grandparents and older relatives. All members of a family had a job to do.

Oregon Trail: Family Roles:
Girls my age cook and mend clothes with our mothers.
My daughter and I mend clothes and cook.
My son and I hunt and fish.
Boys hunt, guard, and fish.

To begin with, the mother was a busy member of the family. She made meals for the family. She also mended clothes. She sewed new clothes and washed them, too.

The father was also an active member of the family. He fished, hunted wild animals, and kept guard of the wagons, campfire, and the animals. He had to keep the cattle, sheep, pigs, and much more safe from wild animals.

The children helped out, too. The boys would help their fathers fix wheels, hunt wild animals, fish, and take care of animals. The girls would help their mothers cook and mend clothes.

Eventually the families got to Oregon. Sadly, some parents, grandparents, friends, and animals passed away on the dangerous trail. But through it all, everyone stayed a family.

The families brought supplies that they would need for the trip.

The families had animals. But sadly they couldn't care for them.

Families in Africa

by Landen

Everyone in an African family has a part to play. Families in Africa might have a mom, dad, kids, grandparents, aunts, and uncles living in the same house. Together these family members make up an extended family.

Moms have hard work to do. They care for the house and family. In big cities, moms might work in offices or as nurses or teachers. They might work in other jobs outside the house, too. In small villages, moms work outdoors growing food to eat.

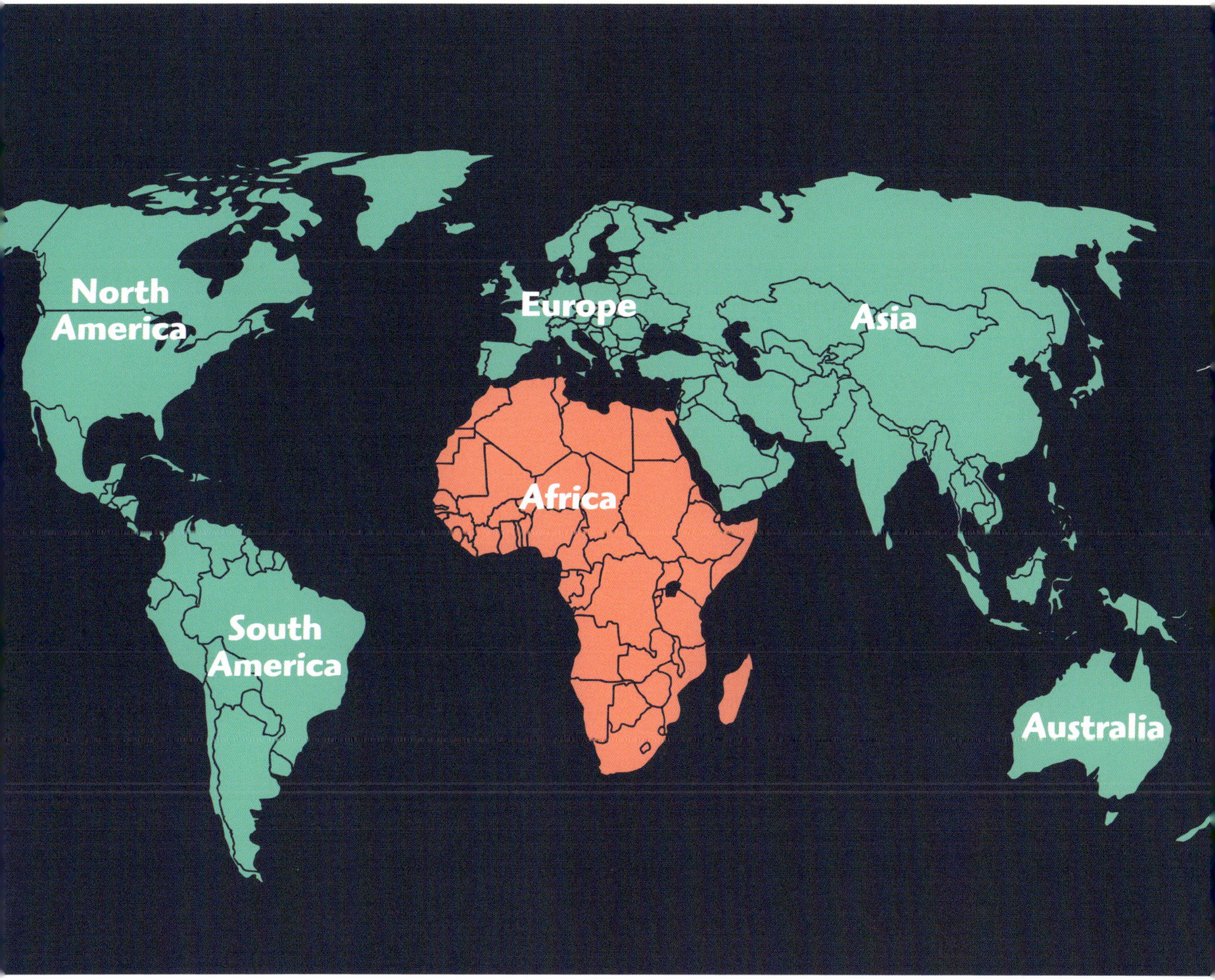
North America
Europe
Asia
Africa
South America
Australia

Dads care for their families in Africa. In big cities, they might work in offices or other jobs outside the house. In small villages, in countries such as Tanzania, dads might hunt for food for the family. Dads also work growing food for their family to eat and to sell to make money.

Kids in African families play a big part. They help clean and cook at home. They might care for younger brothers and sisters. They might work in the fields and help their moms. Many kids in Africa also have to go to school.

Families in Africa work hard. Each member works together to get it all done.

My Family's Roles

by Mia

My name is Mia, and I am 9 years old. I live in Oviedo, Florida. Each person in my family has a different role, but if you put all the roles together we get the job done.

My role in the family is to help my mom. I help her cook. My mom is teaching me how to cook *arroz con frijoles* (rice and beans), *pollo y carne* (chicken and steak), and homemade *helado* (ice cream). I also clean my room, clean the bathroom, and sweep.

My brothers and sisters have roles, too. My brother cleans his room and takes out the trash. He cleans the kitchen with a mop and vacuums the house. He does these chores without being asked. My older sister entertains the baby so he does not make a mess while we are cleaning. She also cleans the dishes. My sister is very helpful. My baby brother does not do much. He eats, naps, and watches TV.

My dad and mom are divorced, but my dad still has a role in our family. He works and earns money. My brothers and sister and I go to his house every weekend.

My mom cooks and helps us with our homework. She cleans and does the laundry, too. My mom likes to keep things neat. She likes the house to be clean and tidy.

My family is unique, but maybe in some ways it is similar to other families. We all have important jobs we have to do.

Pork tacos are a meal some families make together.

illustrated by Jadelynn

A Hardworking Family

by Gabriela

My name is Gabriela, and I live in an apartment in Oviedo, Florida, with my mom, dad, and sister. Like most families, all the people in my family have important jobs to do.

My mom works a lot and cares for us, too. What she makes for dinner is delicious! Sometimes she makes juicy and flavorful *pollo guisado* (rice with chicken stew). When she cleans, the whole house looks brand new, just like when we moved in!

My dad works outside the house at a phone company. My dad is also really proud of what he does to help at home. His role is to clean and cook. He cooks delicious lasagna. When my dad is not cooking, he cleans and organizes the bathroom. He works so much, and he should be proud of that.

Dad's role
who wants lasagna?

My sister works inside and outside the house. She is 21 years old and when she works inside the house she helps my mother clean and cook. My sister also supports me. She compliments my performances, helps me get dressed in the morning, and asks about my grades.

I have a job, too! My role is to go to school, do homework, and clean. My job at school is to learn, pay attention, and to read the homework questions carefully and to show my work. When I clean, I only clean the windows and throw away the trash.

I'm grateful for my family. They make dinner and buy clothes for me. They are also very thoughtful and hardworking. I can tell they love me very much.

I'm throwing away the trash and the trash really Stinks!

My Family

by Eliana

There are many people in my family who all have a job to keep it running. This is a good thing because without my family, I don't know what I would do with myself. They cook and clean and have fun with me. And even though I might be trouble sometimes, they love me and I love them.

Let me tell you about some of my family members. My mom works downtown Chicago in marketing for a food company. When she is home she helps out in the house and keeps working on her marketing job all night until she goes to bed. My dad owns a company that sells lightbulbs. He watches us when our mom works late and sometimes even makes us dinner.

My sister is three years older than I am and is a teenager. This is not a good thing. Once in a while, she plays with me and we make videos together. She helps out in our family by clearing her dishes and putting away the silverware after it is washed.

Smile!
10 more seconds girls!
So much work

I am the youngest child in my family. My job at home is to also clear my dishes and put the silverware away like my sister. I also put away my clothes after they have been washed, and I like to organize my house so that there is no mess.

My aunt (the youngest one, too) is an editor in publishing. She affects my family by coming over once in a while and playing with my sister and me. This might not sound like a job to you but trust me, when you take care of my sister and me, I'm pretty sure that is the toughest job of all. But she still loves being with us.

I am very lucky to have my grandparents nearby. My papa comes over to our house sometimes and fixes things for us. My nana comes over every day of the week to watch my sister and me after school. My other grandma sometimes watches over my sister and me on weekends. She always listens to what we have to say and gives us great advice for the future.

That's our family! As you can see, all of these people are so important to our family. They help us in so many ways and take care of us. I'm so grateful to have them.

Conclusion

by Breckin

Families can be all different sizes and live in different places. No matter where they are in the world or what time in history they lived, all members of a family have responsibilities. Our class researched and wrote about family roles. Now that you've read about them, which family member's role would you like to have?